Properties of Materials

Hot or Cold

Charlotte Guillain

Heinemann Library
Chicago, Illinois

www.heinemannraintree.com
Visit our website to find out more information about Heinemann-Raintree books.

To order:
☎ Phone 888-454-2279
💻 Visit www.heinemannraintree.com to browse our catalog and order online.

Customer Service: 888-454-2279

Visit our website at www.heinemannraintree.com

Designed by Joanna Hinton-Malivoire
Photo research by Elizabeth Alexander
Printed and bound by South China Printing Company Ltd

13 12 11 10 09
10 9 8 7 6 5 4 3 2 1

Library of Congress Cataloging-in-Publication Data

Guillain, Charlotte.
  Hot or cold / Charlotte Guillain.
    p. cm. -- (Properties of materials)
  Includes bibliographical references and index.
  ISBN 978-1-4329-3286-2 (hc) -- ISBN 978-1-4329-3294-7
(pb) 1. Materials--Thermal properties--Juvenile literature. 2.
Heat--Juvenile literature. 3. Cold--Juvenile literature. I. Title.
  TA418.52.G85 2008
  620.1'1296--dc22
                              2008055119

Acknowledgments
The author and publishers are grateful to the following for permission to reproduce copyright material: Alamy pp. **10** (© Aflo Foto Agency), **12** (© Imagestate Media Partners Limited – Impact Photos), **13** (© Tim Gainey), **16** (© Bon Appetit), **19** (© Chris Rout), **21** (© Paul Felix Photography); © Capstone Publishers p. **22** (Karon Dubke); Corbis pp. **9** (© José Fuste Raga/zefa), **14** (© Charles O'Rear); © Corbis p. **17**; iStockphoto p. **6** (© Jon Schulte); Photolibrary p. **18** (Beau Lark/Fancy); Shutterstock pp. **4** (© Thomas Nord), **5** (© Liv Friis-Larsen), **7**, **23** top (© Ronald van der Beek), **8** (© Vera Bogaerts), **11** (© Gary Paul Lewis), **15**, **23** bottom (© SVLumagraphica), **20** (© Sebastian Duda).

Cover photograph of an iceberg reproduced with permission of istockphoto (© Erlend Kvalsvik). Back cover photograph of a woman holding a coffee cup reproduced with permission of Photolibrary (Beau Lark/Fancy).

The publishers would like to thank Nancy Harris and Adriana Scalise for their assistance in the preparation of this book.

Every effort has been made to contact copyright holders of any material reproduced in this book. Any omissions will be rectified in subsequent printings if notice is given to the publisher.

Contents

Hot Materials

Some things can be hot.

Things can change when they are hot.

Hot things can be bright.

Hot things can melt.

Cold Materials

Some things can be cold.

Things can change when they are cold.

Cold things can be hard.

Cold things can be icy.

Hot and Cold Materials

Glass can be hot.
Glass can be bright.

Soil can be cold.
Soil can be hard.

Metal can be hot.
Metal can melt.

Metal can be cold.
Metal can be icy.

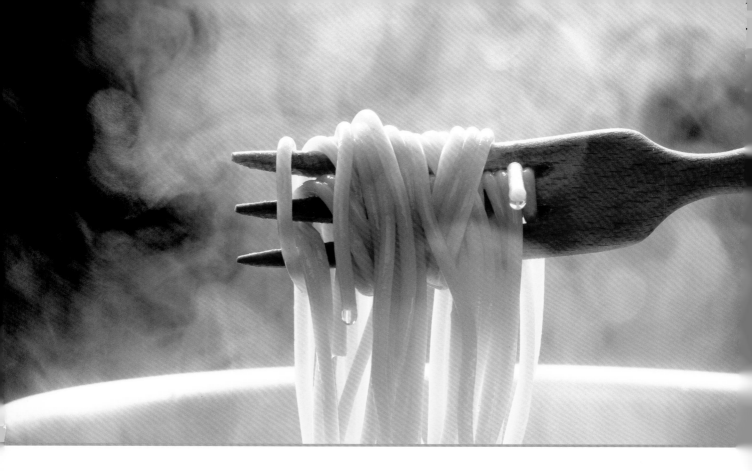

You can tell if something is hot or cold.

You can feel if something is hot
or cold.

Hot things make us feel warm.

Cold things make us feel chilly.

Cold things can get hotter.

Hot things can get colder.

Quiz

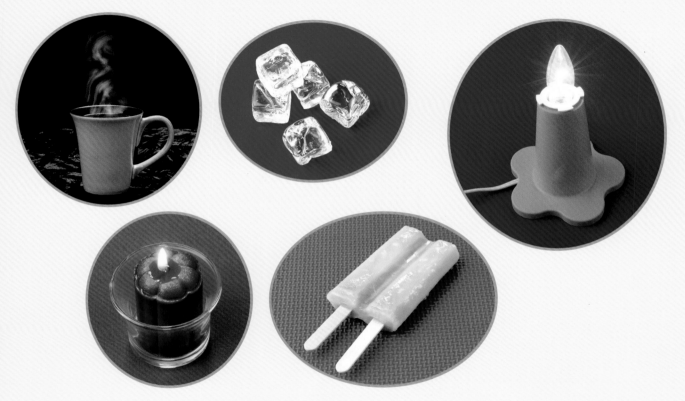

Which of these things are hot?
Which of these things are cold?

Picture Glossary

melt something melts when it becomes soft and runny as it is heated

metal hard, shiny material

Index

Note to Parents and Teachers
Before Reading
Tell children things can be hot or cold. Hot things can melt. Cold things can be icy. Ask children if they know how to tell if something is hot or cold? Can someone give an example of something that melts? What is something that is icy? Show children pictures of hot or cold things. As a class, sort the pictures into groups. As the class sorts the pictures, have children discuss what some of the pictures remind them of. Give children a piece of paper and tell them to fold the paper in half. Have them draw a picture of something hot on one side and something cold on the other side.

After Reading
Place students in small groups. Give each group a clear plastic cup with an ice cube in it. Ask the groups if the object in the cup is hot or cold and how they know that. Have children draw a picture of what the ice cube looks like as soon as they get it. Over the next hour, check on the ice cube and see how it changes. Each time, ask children to record what the ice cube looks like until it turns into water. Once the ice cubes melt, ask the children why they think the ice cube changed.